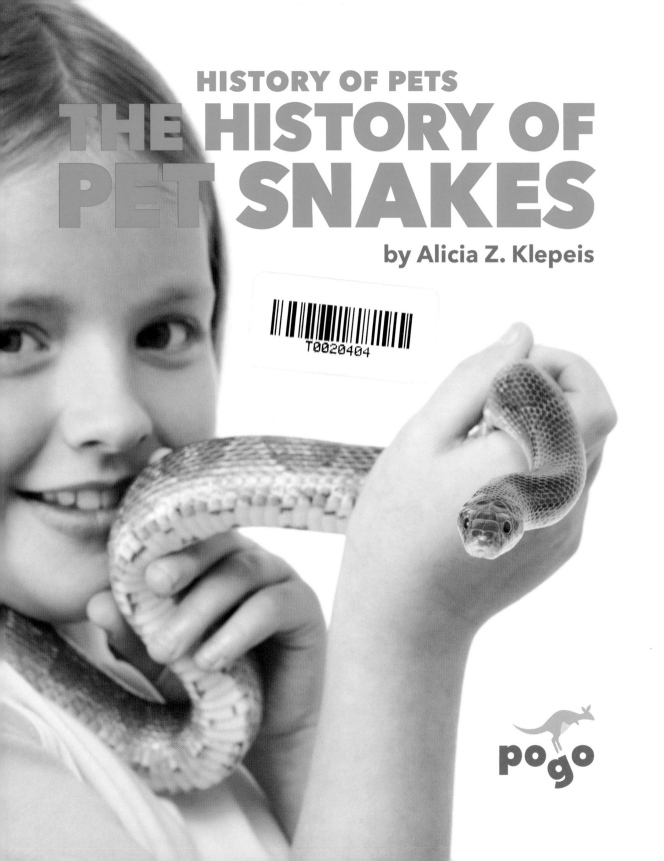

HISTORY OF PETS
THE HISTORY OF PET SNAKES

by Alicia Z. Klepeis

pogo

Ideas for Parents and Teachers

Pogo Books let children practice reading informational text while introducing them to nonfiction features such as headings, labels, sidebars, maps, and diagrams, as well as a table of contents, glossary, and index.

Carefully leveled text with a strong photo match offers early fluent readers the support they need to succeed.

Before Reading

- "Walk" through the book and point out the various nonfiction features. Ask the student what purpose each feature serves.
- Look at the glossary together. Read and discuss the words.

Read the Book

- Have the child read the book independently.
- Invite him or her to list questions that arise from reading.

After Reading

- Discuss the child's questions. Talk about how he or she might find answers to those questions.
- Prompt the child to think more. Ask: Do you have a pet snake or know someone who does? Do you think snakes make good pets? Why or why not?

Pogo Books are published by Jump!
5357 Penn Avenue South
Minneapolis, MN 55419
www.jumplibrary.com

Library of Congress Cataloging-in-Publication Data

Names: Klepeis, Alicia, 1971- author.
Title: The history of pet snakes / by Alicia Z. Klepeis.
Description: Minneapolis, MN: Jump!, Inc., [2024]
Series: History of pets | Includes index.
Audience: Ages 7-10
Identifiers: LCCN 2023006674 (print)
LCCN 2023006675 (ebook)
ISBN 9798885246194 (hardcover)
ISBN 9798885246200 (paperback)
ISBN 9798885246217 (ebook)
Subjects: LCSH: Snakes as pets—Juvenile literature.
Snakes as pets—History—Juvenile literature.
Classification: LCC SF459.S5 K54 2024 (print)
LCC SF459.S5 (ebook)
DDC 639.3/96—dc23/eng/20230510
LC record available at https://lccn.loc.gov/2023006674
LC ebook record available at https://lccn.loc.gov/2023006675

Editor: Eliza Leahy
Designer: Anna Peterson

Photo Credits: Sergey Novikov/Shutterstock, cover; SolStock/Getty, 1, 16; PetlinDmitry/Shutterstock, 3, 23; fivespots/Shutterstock, 4, 22tl; HAPPY EMPEROR/Shutterstock, 5; Artokoloro/Age Fotostock, 6; imageBROKER/G. Lacz/Age Fotostock, 7; Eng101/Dreamstime, 8-9; David McGowen/Adobe Stock, 10-11; Pacific Imagica/Alamy, 12-13 (background); ©John Cancalosi/ard/Age Fotostock, 12-13 (foreground); Juniors Bildarchiv/SuperStock, 14-15tl, 14-15tm, 14-15ml, 14-15 (center), 14-15mr, 14-15bl, 14-15bm, 14-15br, 17; Animals Animals/SuperStock, 14-15tr; SerrNovik/iStock, 18-19; Rozikassim Photography/Getty, 20-21; Nynke van Holten/Shutterstock, 22tr; Eric Isselee/Shutterstock, 22ml, 22mr, 22bl; NatalieJean/Shutterstock, 22br.

Printed in the United States of America at Corporate Graphics in North Mankato, Minnesota.

TABLE OF CONTENTS

CHAPTER 1

STUNNING SNAKES

A snake slithers on the ground as it hunts for **prey** to eat. It flicks its **forked** tongue. Have you ever seen a snake in the wild?

Most snakes are wild. But some people keep them as pets. People often buy them at pet stores. When did people first keep snakes as pets? Let's find out!

CHAPTER 2

SNAKES THROUGH HISS-TORY

People in **ancient** Rome and Greece let snakes live freely in their homes. The snakes ate **pests** such as mice. How do we know? People wrote about them and included them in art.

Ancient Greeks also let snakes roam and hunt in **temples**. The snakes often waited for prey to come close. Then, they would strike. Finally, they swallowed their prey whole.

prey · · · · ▶

four-lined snake

For much of history, people likely kept snakes that were **native** to their area. The snakes in Greek temples were probably four-lined snakes. Some people keep them as pets today.

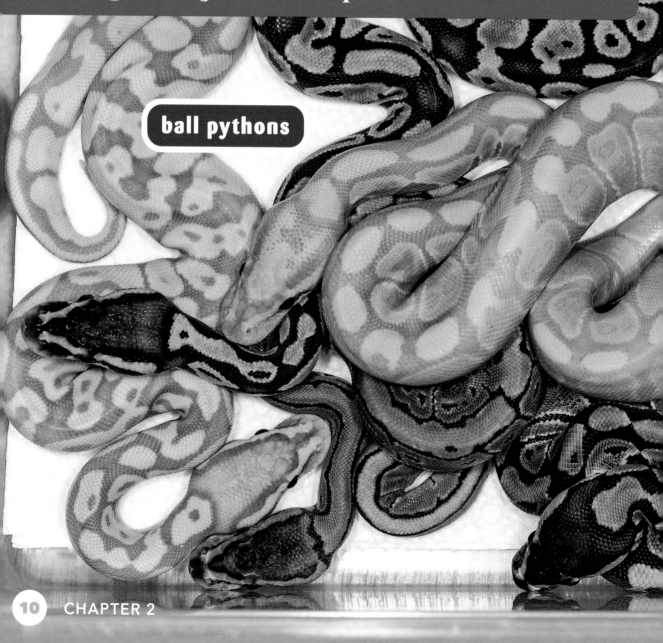

Ball pythons are native to West and Central Africa. In the 1970s, people started capturing them. They **exported** them all over the world. People bought them as pets.

ball pythons

TAKE A LOOK!

More than 3.6 million ball pythons were exported from Africa from 1997 to 2018. Most came from Togo, Benin, and Ghana. Take a look!

MAURITANIA MALI NIGER SUDAN
SENEGAL CHAD
THE GAMBIA BURKINA FASO
GUINEA-BISSAU GUINEA
SIERRA LEONE CÔTE D'IVOIRE NIGERIA
LIBERIA CENTRAL AFRICAN REPUBLIC
GHANA BENIN CAMEROON UGANDA
TOGO EQUATORIAL GUINEA
GABON REP. OF THE CONGO
Atlantic Ocean DEMOCRATIC REPUBLIC OF THE CONGO RWANDA BURUNDI TANZANIA
ANGOLA ZAMBIA

– – – ball python native range

People often buy snakes at pet stores. Within the last 50 years, it has become much easier to buy **exotic** snakes.

Pet owners want snakes that can live in cages. They also want snakes that are easy to handle. Because of this, many snakes are **bred** to be **docile**.

WHAT DO YOU THINK?

If too many exotic snakes are taken from their native homes, their numbers in the wild could suffer. Do you think it is right to take animals out of the wild? Why or why not?

corn snake
morphs

Pet snakes are bred to have different colors or patterns. Corn snakes are naturally orange or brownish-yellow. But breeders have created hundreds of **morphs**.

CHAPTER 3

FRIENDS WITH SCALES

About 2 million Americans have pet snakes. People like snakes for many reasons. They come in many colors and patterns. They are quiet. They are fun to watch. But pet snakes are a lot of work.

heat lamp

Most need heated cages. Why? They are **cold-blooded**. Owners must feed snakes dead animals, like mice, that they buy online or at pet stores. Some people hide food in puzzle boxes or mazes. It gives the snakes exercise. It also challenges their brains.

Snakes can recognize people. Some experts think it is possible for pet snakes to **bond** with people. Some snakes seem to like being held. They may rub their heads against their owners. Some even loop their body around a person's neck or shoulders.

WHAT DO YOU THINK?

Many kinds of pets bond with their owners. Do you think the bond between a person and an animal is different than the bond between people? Why or why not?

Some pet snakes can live for more than 30 years. That is a long time to get to know one another! Would you like a pet snake?

QUICK FACTS & TOOLS

1. ball python

2. corn snake

3. red-tailed boa

4. California kingsnake

5. rosy boa

6. milk snake